Mountain Meadow Amore

Rub -
A DIFFERENT LOOK -
HOPE THIS ONE HARMONIZES
W/ SOM OF THOSE GOOD
COUNTRY BTRCAPS.

BEST,
Benny

Mountain Meadow Amore

Sonny Gratzer

Writers Club Press
San Jose New York Lincoln Shanghai

Mountain Meadow Amore

All Rights Reserved © 2000 by Sonny Gratzer

Writers Club Press
an imprint of iUniverse.com, Inc.

For information address:
iUniverse.com, Inc.
5220 S 16th, Ste. 200
Lincoln, NE 68512
www.iuniverse.com

ISBN: 0-595-15776-9

Printed in the United States of America

In memory

of

beautiful ladies.

Epigraph

"I want to do with you what spring
does to the cherry trees."

Pablo Neruda
from
Every Day You Play,
Twenty Love Poems and a
Song of Despair

Table of Contents

Preface

One of life's great joys is to admire women. I like women. I like their shapes, whims, looks, laughs, troubles, kindnesses, and their flirtations, nearly everything about them. Of course, there is often a downside, but it is too boring to contemplate.

I have especially cared for a few women very much. Some of them I have written of, to and about in the stories within these covers. I did not attempt to define each of them from the other, but I tried to glorify who and what they are to me. Nothing more immediate or complex than that. I like them.

I like these women very much. Still. And will. The problems that evolved in these relationships are not matters to worry about. Only the excitement each caused.

Am I being egotistical? Of course I am. I mean to be, otherwise why write these things, and especially why publish them? Make of it what you will, wise reader, but know that I meant every word, for my sake and theirs.

I also wanted to write another book like this to supplement my first effort in this genre: *General Issue Blues, Viet Nam to Here: A Warrior's Tour*. It is a legacy, as I do not expect to leave much else. That is, nothing is so finite as a book of words to be read as testimony to parts of a life. I want to leave something to which my offspring can point as something their father/grandfather did, something not quite like anything anyone else did. These words, linked as I made them, are mine alone. So, perhaps a bit of spite is interlocked with pride, maybe to shock doubters a bit. There are those who remember me locked into the physical side of life as warrior, fighter, player and struggler. I do enjoy music and other art forms, and I do know and appreciate the finer, softer side of life. This as much as anything is why I want to publish these pieces.

I am self-centered enough to want you to read and like these poems, to find something of yourself in them, and to read them to your lovers.

All of you won't have the background of beautiful Montana as a fountainhead to supplement your seductive moves, but you can't have everything.

Sonny Gratzer
September, 2000

Acknowledgements

I offer an inadequate and pithy statement of thanks to my daughter, Dana Gratzer Millhouse, for being an astute reader, to old friend and advisor, Printer Bowler, to Rich Snell, my computer guru and Webmaster, and especially to you lovely ladies who exist forever in these pages. You know who you are.

Mountain Meadow Amore is Sonny Gratzer's second book of poetry, following *General Issue Blues, Viet Nam to Here: A Warrior's Tour.*

Mountain Meadows

A blend of spirits free as our own
Begs for mixture in the same suspiration
Inhaled and absorbed in a long breath.

Years of divergence merge in our mountain
     meadows high.
Prophetic images spill from a shared cup.
Our vessels tip and spill precious life juices
In our high green mountain meadows.

Sweet grass of mountains high
I crawl through to you.
My worth, my life, is a value if you allow me
To kneel and kiss your sugar feet,
Your huckleberry ankles, your honey thighs.

I am your supplicating slave.
I bind myself to your needs.
I give you me.

You are my purple blossom,
A beautiful bitterroot
From my mountain meadow.

I live to share you.
Having you is my life's pursuit.

I kneel in the sweet high mountain grass before you.
You are the path to my kingdom.
You are the wonder of my dreams.
You are my alpine meadow, and I live in your
     sweetness

Nightly.

When We Sleep

Where do you go when you are tired,
When your eyes flutter asleep?
Do you enter my world, read my books,
Paint my colors, salute my flags?
Where do you go?
Do you visit my ebony neck,
My mahogany back,
Do you pick my flat-wrapped strings?
Do you sing the meadowlark's song in your sleep,
The sweetest bird song of all?
Does my brilliant peacock tail
Attract you when you sleep?
When I drag my tired feet;
Do you let me lean on you?
If my lips dry in the night,
Do you kiss them?
If I meander in my dreams,
Do you follow on tiptoe?
When I look back for you,
Are you there when we sleep?

Sonny Gratzer

Out of Season

I wilt in memory of your last night with me
When you strove to withdraw
For fear of marring your landscape.
Be alert to my strong-arm
Tactics when next we meet. I will be bent
On disarming you, of bending your will.
I want you with me always. And when I win, beware.
I will leave you when snow blurs my windows.
I am not trustworthy in frigid air.
I have no shame for being weak.
I am a coward in the face of loving women.
I need to hide, to desert, to go AWOL.
I am a coward in the face of female artillery.
I can't face you when you are strong.
Return; teach me to fight, to conquer you,
To ignore your negative response to me.
It's merely a game of seasons.
Do what you want with me.
Do you want me to go in the blizzard?
I can make snow angels in this game.
I will play with mittens and snow forts.
I will leave as you desire, only tell me so
With great heaves of truth in Winter's breath.
Save your face from freezing.
Bulldoze me with warm truth.
Skydive with gales of trust.
Trek with truth in freezing temperatures.
Tell me. I will forgive your reticence,
Your negative being, your lack of desire for me.

Mountain Meadow Amore

I will deal with it in the Spring.
Blow me over.
Bury me deep.
Sweet sugar Fall days light the orange
Glow of truth and birch leaves
And red berries of Summer's Mountain Ash.

Trial

A single sand grain casts a greater shadow of
    hope than you give me.
Your hot eyes burn my thoughts, my skin, my
      heart.
We are headed nowhere. We are not complete.
My eyes grow cold as windblown glaciers.
Cold permeates me since you departed with
    your hot eyes.
Your warm sensuous lusting self
Sees my feet sliding over slippery pine needles in
      the trail
To your mouth. My mouth grows to yours as
      deeply rooted trees
Grow in rich black forest soil. I would dip my
      fingers in acid
Were they to become more sensitive to your skin.
They could not be more responsive to your
      heated body, so I dream.
It is thoughtless to want you more than you
      want me.
I put you on trial. I find you guilty as charged
But there is no sentence.
You are justified.
You are just, and justice wins.

Your Prize

Soft shadows of fading greens
Tranquilize my receding envy.
Charging grizzlies would not fight
Harder were your prize extant.
Pros and cons weighted
Against your fruitful life
Show my niggardliness contrasted.
Misdirected lives won't connect in time
For fruition normally counted.
Minimal offerings take up the slack.

Sonny Gratzer

Windows Closed

Our eve closed, our newness blunted.
What caused your loss of love, the end of joy?
Tipped lamps and crooked fingers
Point back in dim glows of buried love
And futures passed in golden hair.
The promise was great,
Gave tender joy we nearly redeemed
However short-lived.
Perpetual love lives deep inside,
A dream better left there waiting
The shaft from Cupid's bow
Remembering those wishes long ago,
Words borrowed from cross and key.
My Muse lives in you yet,
However much you and I disguise
What we once wanted.
I miss you.
I've missed you since you said my name,
Since you leaped to kiss me
In that
Homecoming moment,
Since the forests thickened
And your tender skin felt my rough edges.
The window is closed
But not locked.

Three-Way Musings

Veins copperheaded blue and gold.
Memories of family hold me.
Sunshine, clean air, fresh water, swimming.

Wishful isn't true thinking, the times long past.
    History is pure and reality neglected.
What is life, something new? Remembrances are
    good.
    Life is good, isn't it?
Sunflowers, vacuous minds, holding all things good.

Die, don't we? If not, spin the wheel, go again.
Pretend we live and go once more.
Give me a time machine, and when it's time to recycle
    Let me go back in time and get full value for it?
    Hardly.
Rainbows assured, lightning bolts in reality appear.
    Where are the thunderclouds?

Your Glistening Self

I hate myself for reasons I can't tell you.
Your soft side could not take the truth I know.
Someday you'll learn how much I care for you
But I must give you more time to grow.

Your glistening self deceives me,
Encourages belief in something not there.
Bristling cold of October wind
Hits like your reflections.

You don't call them that.
You think of fairness and honesty and openness.
I feel the hurt, the wind blowing
Through chimes meant for spring and hope.

Mandolins sweetly played ache my husk
Of a body, my small words
Meant to mean much laying flat, airless.
Your revenge, not erased, is endless.

Your sweet glistening self, your resolve
Is not meant as your façade,
But you withhold,
Enjoying us for yourself, unshared.

My body's failing, my mind's aglow,
So what I feel inside you have a right to know.
I care for you deeply but ill, I can't commit
When life seems short and unknown to the end of it.

Reflections

Yellowing corn plant leafs reflect,
Merging,
Party to my pain.
Early wrapped Christmas gifts
Exceed my authority
To live longer,
Disguised as expectations.
Wasted wishes get crack-blocked,
Blind-sided by my karma.
Winter's sadness is settling in.
Stiffening my aching neck,
Increasing the blows.
Corn doesn't grow now so why worry
About the heart's sunlight?

Waging Lover's War

My xylophone puffs deep,
Deep ambrosial smells
Through your flimsy tissue defenses.
I am teak strong to your balsa.
You have no hope.
I will overcome your wistful play
At defending against me.
You want to wage futile war.
Your errors made
Believing it possible?
You can't win.
I am tuned to the War God of Love.
She hovers on my shoulder
Warning of your deceit.
I listen and I win.
I don't listen and I lose.
Swinging swiftly, licking low,
A Ranger in danger
I wander nightly, freshly,
Eager for the fictile fray.
Engage me
Or not.

Delicacy

Wind wisps, so lithe they seem airless.
Texture's smells linger sensuously
When you lick my fingers whole.
Let me smell you.
Let me taste you.

You are a morsel,
A treat to eat.
You are delicious
As lemon yogurt.
Let me taste you.

You are a special burger
Wrapped in sweet onion.
Your mustard is sweet
As warm bee honey.
Let me taste you.

Your tangy red pizza sauce
Drips from my kissed lips
Scorched by jalapeno juice
And saucy pepperoni.
Let me taste you.

Tidbits of tiny bites of you
Linger with your smell.
Your scent left itself
In my shopping bag of dreams.
Let me taste you.

Was It Wine and Not Love?

How long it has been
Since we shared the same room?
I watched you on the steps
Wiping tears.
Pictures taken, songs sung,
I walked to you without seeing others.
Stepped back to look.
Your eyes still filled
With misty sorority songs.
I wasn't sure you knew me.
Your hair, bright and short,
Clothes immaculate,
Beautiful and groomed.
I mentally checked myself
Trying to see myself through your eyes.
Would I pass?
You, a sight, small,
Looking up, glistening.
I wanted to hold you there.
So many eyes aware of our hug.
We sat alone on a brick retaining wall,
Measuring, remembering,
Laughing, searching,
Touching—finally escaping.
Short night, long memories,
Sweet dreams, pleasant smells,
Distant calls,
Bittersweet
Romance.
Rue!

Alone With You Again

Peach florets
    crown your soft brow.
You are for me
    the cream of life.
Our sweet life,
    our good sweet life.

Matchless souls are spread
    by time and circumstance,
by facts of life,
    yours so complete and pressed,
mine physically wrinkled
    by strife and war.

By my own damnation!

Hell can't be worse.
    Songs are somewhere sung for us,
harmonizing us,
    being us.
So fleeting,
    these precious moments with you.

Pitter-Patter

Exigencies in airport lounges
Produce fleeting lover's contact.
Pitter-patter tears, we say,
Teenagers again, rousing what-ifs.
Our retained enthusiasm is a year old
Sustained by too-short calls,
Suffused with enabling tinkling
Chimes of your laughter.
A good sign!
Soul mates!
Veneration!
Long distance intricacies
Lack the enamoredness of shared life.
Pitter-patter.

Lake Nymph

Languid pale-dusky skin
So smooth my eyes ache.
Your brow furrows in thought
Oblivious to your radiant skin.
I want to touch it. To kiss it.
To feel it. To stroke it.
It gives me pleasure, your skin.
My hands warm from its radiance.
Heat-warming inner strength
Strong as your slender thighs.
Your yellow-white hair half wet,
The bottom half, from lake water,
Formed in African ringlets.
Brown glasses hide your eyes
But I know you're watching me.
I know. I know.

Hanging Thoughts

Healthy inscribed guillotines hanging high
Serve salmon caught at midnight rodeos.
Rosettes and Pearls of Mother to Be
Merge with wives and lovers who leave me,
Promising me well in the iron lung of stifling life.
With lifelines severed plastic ends
Crumble in passion, twisting ends
Of falling flame—a dead zone.
Mahogany strips show evidence of
Tight pursed lips rouged in fire.
Fans scream in high-powered engines taking flight.
Plaid fields below fancy tight streamlined
Bowlines tethering us to this earthly plane.
We can't get off.
We are staked.
Hearts bleed and tears flow.
We are stopped in bear tracks.
We inveigh critics to be not harsh.
Please be kind.
Don't judge. Give us what we want.
We pray and beg, often the same thing.
August heat fries skillet streets and cowboy fairs
Turn Ferris wheels into Viking food.
Your yearning shows and it hurts my spine.
I clamor for freedom, afraid of treated
Railroad ties too heavy to lift,
Too strong to break.
We are staked!
The façade is you believe me.

Mountain Meadow Amore

How strange. You believe anything.
Why? Look! Look at me!
You are fooled. Do I fool you so easily?
Yes, but you fool you too
When we meet in our trysting place.

Cuts

Scarred landscapes carved in red soil
Glisten in bouncing white beads
Deeply sliced in her self.
She retched great pouring spouts of crimson
Between stitched memories of vital battles.
Her eyes withheld pain from me
But allowed submission, fears and love
To show, granting me her ache and repression.
I could not express adulation. The rancid smell of its
Mottled valley is destructive in its acridity.
Death is sweeter living next to emulous putrefaction.
Her kindness killed me, bled me to death.
She belched volcanoes of stench.
She sent me to my personal hell
Where I'm consigned to live with maggots
Feasting on what is left of myself.

Dew Drops

I feel your name passing in thunder.
I quiet the emerald seas in a vigorous land.
Your lasting smell lingers longer than dew in the valley
In spring; in mountain meadows covered by
     wild honeysuckle
I stretch my yearning arms to wrap Grizzly-
     scratched yellow pine
I know you hid behind when I searched for you
     on the hill.
I run to catch your name in the wind.
I know it's there, waiting to be said,
Glistening wet falling from the heavens,
Dripping from bushes in hidden places
Where old ladies secret their favorite huckle-
     berry haunts.
Speckled mushrooms blacken in the moss
Where bears roll in cushioned comfort.
I wait for your moist eyes to look at me with love,
With lost-and-found yearning and hope its tone
     is alto deep
When you sing, matching great low rumbling thunder.

Sonny Gratzer

My Wishful Thinking

The night is bleak but full
In the belly of my wishful thinking,
Programmed with maybes and wonder-ifs.
I keep my feet off the ground with interest
To play the game, to prevent surprise.
I think too much but it prepares me,
Even if never needed.
One can't prepare enough.
We will our space with expanded memories
Of wishful thinking.
The fall, the plunge, the drop is deadly,
Especially when it is unexpected.
I will land, aimed where I need to land
Even if I go it alone to the damned end.

Thank Heaven the Nights Grow Longer

Raw emotion stiffens spines
Dripping wet in secluded splendor.
Surf syncopates with my deck chimes,
An erratic earth's heat beat.
In the wee September hours
Embers comfort me in night's chill.
Spider's web spun Chinese Checkers across my lamp.
Last evening's honkers sounded friendly notes
In search of night resting places
During their season's drawing southward journey.
Other northern neighbors remain ensconced
Waiting winter's chill by firesides.
All to what end, an incessant search for love,
For mating, for securing places?
Be like me. Drift aimlessly, inwardly.
The journey is the same—a repetitive flap hither
        and yon.
We all come back here, wherever here is.
A downside always exists
But only naysayers flout it with death wishes.
The nights grow longer.
Thank heaven we have more time
To savor short sunlit blazes.

Send It To Me

Send it to me as you would to your other lover.
Let me have your lips full as he gets them.
Intertwine in your limbs and fingers as grace-
    fully with me
As I know you do otherwise.
Torment me.
Ease my mind.
Lie to me.
Send it to me as you would were he not there.
The cliff is high and steep; don't let me fall.
Hold me with your strength, your strong fingers.
Let your hair fall to me as I hang free; swing
    me gently.
Don't let me fall.
Send it to me, your true love, your only love.
Forget him.

Influence

Quandaries abound breathed to life
    By my own intransigence.
I worship your weeded self,
    Even your sweet tiny fingers.
Others wish for me, ask for me
    Fervently and I quake.
I wait. I wait for you still
    Knowing the differences.
There are many.
    Are we in love with being in love?
Others in our sphere wonder
    And worry more for me than you,
Convinced of my shameless cuckolding.
    We do it together, freely.
You live with your friend
    And think of your lover.
Are you in too deep? Is my quandary yours?
    Do we provoke short-term problems
With no long-term plans?
    Speculate, tiny fingers, think ahead.
Climb your mountains, cross your seas,
    Visit castles, complete your mission.
Finish your driven quest. Does it end?
    Do you satitate yourself?
Some beauty is lost in the eye of the beholder
    When dead ends meet.
Give me that bit to hold, that tiny finger
    Bit of life to live on.

Help From the Little Ones

You walk on soft pink lilac petals strewn by wee folks frolicking ahead
Who wait for the fragrance released by your soft rending toes.
Your sun-tinted hair lights their faerie way even in bright days.

You radiate goodness and cheer in the wee one's wakes
While following the little people to their favorite bear's lair.
I am your bear. I eat little people, especially you.

You are succulent and sweet and good and warm and wet.
I need to nuzzle, to make you wetter, to warm my hands and mouth
In your warmth and wetness. You need it and I want you to want it.

Think of the scent and sight of our bubble, the small part
Of the planets we inhabit: lilacs crushed, skin warm and radiating, hair
The color of sunset, mouths pursuing each other, hands reaching, fingers

Digging, love responding, love responding …love responding …
Our love for each other responding to our responding to our responding.
The little ones know. They help in our secret quest,
Hiding in my lair.

Invasion

Gains elude me while I plan the invasion of you, my Normandy.
The task is daunting as I am troopless and will go it alone.
No one helps me into your gunnels, into your Higgins.
Your shoreline obstacles are difficult to overcome.
No going around them, you set them so brilliantly.
Your nests of guns so well hidden I can't destroy them.
Your mounds of pillboxes so formidable I can't destroy them.
Your landmines so covertly placed I can't destroy them
Except
By using my body as a detonator,
As a missile,
As a bangalore torpedo.
I will make the breach.
Count on it.

Talking With My Hands

You responded so well.
I spoke so low, soft times,
Yet you heard me.
The whisper was soft,
Easy, rippling.
Yet you heard me.
Sparklers light the lake
With dancing rays from
Midnight skies.
Big winds remind us
Who is in charge
When the lights are out.
Your eyes loomed large,
Expressive,
Especially enhanced
By lovemaking and wet games.
You are a modeled sight
And I should be near you.
I need to walk beside you
Head held high with pride,
High and true the day though.
Kissing you, your arms around me
The mode is set and the lake is wet,
And sparkles light it yet.

Edges

Why do you watch tolerantly
    When I rant through tears
    At crooked lines?
Bad drivers vent on me
    When I'm in their way
    But you give me space.
You are a subtle benefactress
    Whom I owe more than trinkets
    I owe my soul. Your aura is a halo.
Angels decide how you live, and where.
    My wings are clipped;
    You fly free.
Swans bend elongated necks your way
    With a smooth nod to entwine
    Us as lovers. We emulate them.
My bear is grizzled; your faerie is light and free.
    You jump nimbly to touch neon;
    I rise high reaching with claws.
Oyster shells slip through the screen
    You hold for me;
    I know how to get through.

    I know how to get through.

My Blue Heaven

Heaven's dust sprinkles from your flashing eyes.
Your lips shine comet's blood red in my sphere.
Your radiant skin shines beams through my nerves.
Shimmering butterfly wings mount steel horses
Causing thickened vines to sweat steam in heated pores.

Encores delay suspended on eternal signals.
New matches ignite pairings unfulfilled,
Yearning, yearning for winter's end,
For mid-summer's single night together
Between sheets of unabated wet weather.

Long for me, my budding delight.
Long for us, for our-soon-to-be night.
Long for those lost days we gave away.
Long for returns in new memories made.
Together once, for hours few, for creating lifelong dreams anew.

Special wines are foreign for me, as are places you hurry to see.
My special time is familiar in place and count.
I demand nothing new, no cries in the night,
No pleading to be there when we can't make it right.
Only the wish for you to be with me in my blue heaven.

June's end meets July's start, of intent unseen, kept apart.
Leave the bad and come to the art of mountain meadowland.
Slowly wind your fingers around what last you only guessed about,
Pretending we knew nothing of what it was we wanted.
Back to me, for once, no traces there, or here, of our deep hearts.

Mythic Sails

Incessant pounding wakes my soul
Turning into wrinkled bowl peaches.
No wine drunk in the endless night
While midnight sloops slip by in ghostly silence.
A gnarled driftwood mustard spoon adorns my table.
Cobbled bridges support my path crossing your stream.
I sense through chirping fish hawks.
I hear pained squeals in windblown streaks.
I touch wispy clouds in your brow
Feeling desperate laughter in your bones.
I don't treat you in submerged thought as you treat me.
I taste storms blood red when you wrestle indiscriminate
Thoughts in sun's nestling orange plunge.
Flattened weeds kissed by seagull bomb runs to embellish our shores.
Saying grace, meaning it ever more with weekends earned
By happy faces boiling in the rum pot.
Save to the last—yet be first to give—
Riding your sailboat of dreams.

Dried Tears

Tears washed fill channels
In your languorous neckline.
Can I taste such icy drops,
Those salt crusts
When I get there, dried,
Not for me but for your past
And future loves?
We all share bits of these lives.
More to love and live,
More to lick and laugh.
Love comes from in here.
From in here.

My Empty Hands

Lines sought by my eyes found your hips flaring tiny and smooth,
Perfect gifts for my hands.
Grateful grazing, these eyes of mine. They absorb you.
Your tiny mouth fits my loud braying Slavic kind.
Your tiny hands smothered by mine send great inward strength.
Your tiny feet pad brightly next to my slowed war-made gait.
You forget to slow for me, padding ahead, then realize I'm behind.
We walk hand in hand, but I feel my awkward moves
Transfer through my hands to you.
I am not made for you.
Your strength and grace leave my bulk ashamed.
Your misty eyes lock on mine.
Wordlessly you send I'm sorrys.
You turn to leave;
I feel your warm hips for the last time,
Their determined move leaving my hands empty.

Harmony

Your ageless grace is kept trim
With work and hard love and high hikes.
Daisies in your hair
Are tucked for me to pluck.
My skin is your skin.
My touch is your touch.
My soul is enriched
By sand squeezed through your toes on the beach.
The water I feel is your liquidness flowing through me.
Your angel kisses are my marks from before.
Your chords chime in harmony
With the whistle I blow on your neck.
You smell like that just for me.
I am brown against your white for your attention.
You breaststroke to my mouth to converge.
I give you me with fervor.
You hold my heart
In your young memory and old future.

Thinking in the Rain

My cheeks blot smothered lips painted bright
In ways I dislike, as I'm not made for make-up.
Phones keep ringing, not my calls, but why?
Talk is flimsy and goes nowhere so why lament
What can't be changed, what can't be done?
Pretend that all's well, barriers declivitous,
That other minds won't stop loud thinking.
Seldom seen love inside rain drops
Cools my ardor even as enveloping sunshine
Dissipates drizzled plops on my head shield.
Schmoozing calls reconcile my guard's-up stance
Some moments before I share the load.

Together

At times being born again is stifling.
My missions radiate from distant stars
Defining me to you.
You fail to see me, to understand me.
I see you. I intuit you. I know you.
You hold back.
Why?
It's a tale long told by soldiers, and often.
From acorn covered trees to corn in the fields,
You devour me; I feed you.
I have fed you for centuries.
We have always been together.
We have always been apart.
This is how we fit, our totality.
A spoon of rice.
We are whole beef flesh.
We are mother's milk.
We never will be,
We always will be
Lovers.

A Cry in the Night

Spent youth lies roadside
Worn from the goads of energy spent.
Yet your skin glowed that night,
A soft golden hue in the dim autumn light.
Your tummy arched with thrusted sighs
With perfect angle for my lusting eyes.
Your smiling lips extend
With ringing chimes of yeses
Your voice sang soft and high as a child's
High pitch belying your fifty years.
Peach florets thrust mouthward
Wet and sweet and good,
Petals unlocking your golden gate
Ever wide, begging for more.

Would You?

Would you allow me to live in your eyes?
There is room, alongside sweet loving mist.
I propel myself deeper to find your soul.
I would massage you from inside, closer than before.
Closer than anyone.
I would prop you on your elbows to gaze steady,
Me looking out—and in.
I would have it both ways.
I would love you.
I would love you
Deeper and more intensely than anyone.
But I dream.
Would you dream with me?
Such freedom exists.
Is it in you?
Would you explore?
Would you grin with happy eyes, chin propped on your hands,
Elbows propped, grin deep in my grin?
Would we grin inside each other?
Would you give it up?
Would you find the happiness you need?
Would I?
Dare we?
My sleepless nights would be yours.
I would massage you from without.
Robins in my wormfull yard would be happy.
The worms would be happy to give themselves to the robins.
Your breasts would blush.
I would massage them.

We would be passionate and would share.
I would unlock your dreams.
You would read to me.
I would learn from you.
Cherries would blossom early.
The crop would be expansive.
Each bud would have its own dream,
Its own set of robins and worms,
Its own territory to massage.
I would give it to you.
You would smile at me inside
With those unique happy misty eyes.

To Love Away

You shine in silent prose typewritten
    to avoid my sluggish hand.
You punctuate impatient commas
    following recorded slants in my life.
You hex me with exclamations of loyalty
    while remaining judiciously aloof.
You break my bones with lower case "luv,"
    sedulous in distant tease.
You capitalize on questions, period,
    while I am a hyphenate.
Chapters new will be written future tense
    when we learn the tense we're in.

Giggles in the Rain

Splendiferous memories of your repose
Liberate you from your usual cosmos.
Laying with me during midnight's falling,
The two of us naked and intertwining.
You giggle in my mind's eye
As I see you looking at a rainy night sky.
Sometime we'll be together again other than in
      memory's lane
At a time I can stay with you through the rain
      and late hours again,
To drive shiny highways holding your hand
For real rather than in my own dreamland.

Where Do I Go?

Winter-Spring winds chill my hardened bones
While the Snake's mist settles below Stewart's crown.
White smudges plaid northern towering white pines.
I think of you trekking high in the Alps, the Andes,
The Sierras, while I stare at brilliant Rockies' crusts.
Where would I tread were I able?
All's hidden in alpine forests, if not lost.
Early day sent me lakeside, drifting
In self-imposed solitude.
I glide through the high alpine valleys,
The Missions greeting me on the Ravalli rise,
The Snake's mist reaching north amid
MacDonald's towering crest.
My silence breaks with siren's wailing toward the wreck.

Feckless

Wind blast makes
fingers pinch
when spring's storm
from winter lingers.
Swept through fretted notes
carved by plastic picks,
my loving sounds float
with she-loves-me, she-loves-me-not
daisy petals falling in my
grassy field of love for you.
Burgundy red deep conviction
pours from the slashing sheen
I bleed for you.
My heart pumps speeding
knots, hurting, dreaming.
I wait for your answer…
Chords blend, suspended 4ths
arouse my expectations,
  my dreams
    my wishes.
     I
      dream
       too
        hard.

Mountain Chivalry

Garlands festoon sungold lanes
Where I lay my cape justifying rain.
Soggy threats strung taut above
In shapes of interwoven Old Man clouds.
Wreathes are plentiful in this great Northwest
Where I lay my cloth of love to express
To you when flowers wilt without your toe
Touching the weave of the uncommon bough.
The sun grows bold, breaks up the grim
Start of the day, sun streaking in.
Even if rain darkens the time,
For you, my love, I'll lay a bouquet.

Wild Calling

You convey coyote howls my way, wilderness lady.
Elk bugle and your passions scream to me.
Something echoing triumphantly peels my frown away.
You soothe my brow with whispered lips blowing warmly.
Glacier peaks tower from your heaving chest,
Breathing in my listening part, closing my eyes
To see your glistening eyes teasing
Through sounds of breezes billowing through our bower.
Spread your meadows of mirthful charm
On nature's wish, on our coupling love.
When I fool you, when you are disarmed,
Believing when time's right, I'll lay down my glove.

A Vessel Leaking

Sentences stultified my candor for you
Long before I stated true
How stifling life's been without you.
I wrote those words long ago
In hopes to pour truths for you
From a vessel leaking.
I locked myself to the idea
Of finding the one love with whom to spend an era,
A timeless course to love the special soul you are,
Poured from my vessel leaking.

Tindery Love

Tindery is our love,
Dried in draught
What was heated
Sucked our marrow's
Thin vein of coolant.
We tried too hard.
We shamefully
Neglected to irrigate.
We let fields run dry.
Tindery love,
Dry as Fall's leaves
Finger crushed.
Blazes create
Potential pother.
Pray for moisture, a thunderstorm,
Tender blessings
Balm our tindery love.

Look the Other Way

Far too long my duplicity carried me
Then I found honesty with lovers to be more hurtful.
I evolve, change, decide,
Then equivocate, look sideways,
Then I hurt—deep troubling soulful pain—
I smile.
Actually.
I smile.
I don't know why.
I do it at funerals and death.
I do it with dissolving loves.
I do not find it funny.
Incongruous, perhaps.
My payback? My redemption? Black humor?
Definitely not comedy,
Not laughs, not fun.
I am wrongfully thought to be hard, harsh.
That case can be made.
In love, I am both close and distant.
I am generous and stingy.
I give and take away.
I am afraid.

Wanton Memories

Red webs spun in dawn flush my desire
To lay next to you in sleep.
Thin stitches hold iron racks tight to your breasts.
Flechettes shot from fountains of the young
Pierce memory's otherwise bland torture.
Metered numbers give credence to my conquests.
Would that you were one.
Would you become one?
You could become three hundred and one.
I intuit my wasted youth but lack secure knowledge.
When will I know better?
Ice caps grown on mountains are licked by your radiance.
Your pressing heat sucked jungles dry to desert
Now laid burnt next to infertile salmon
Drowned in dam's wash.
Why do you wear hats?
To keep your beauty from rising
When you beat dust from my rugs.
I suffer from champagne's jade.
I mean nothing.
I am spent.
Cemeteries should be barren of cold souls,
Become places of mirth and joy,
Not sullen holes of rot.
Where are you old friends?
Where are you family?
Claim golden shadows on my brow.
Give back your lost memory.

Responses

You rippled my thoughts,
Massaged me in eucalyptic splendor
While angels whispered our names.
Myrtle merged our sweat
And sweeter juices.
Where is there a kinder touch?
Your fingers were gentle,
Soft on my aching self.
Reach the limits when you want.
Fear nothing in response.
Release totally,
Abandon your obtrusion,
Self-imposed.

The Dance Ending

Dances end precisely
When flames die.
Neighboring states support
My crumbling hillside.
Calcified love affairs aren't revived
Passing reviewing stands.
Saber salutes, though shiny and smart,
Gleam with dull blades.
Mondays on the streets of pain
Lack love and connection.
You smirk at my failures,
Pursed and puckered.
We are not synchronized,
Your lies stabbing and slashing,
Digging for my fluids the color of your lips.
Death comes slowly to devious loves
Dissolving in sweet cotton candy bits,
Hollow and empty.
We dance around the question
Watching the candle flicker.

Sonny Gratzer

Velvet Hammer's Blow

Tonight I feel ownership
Of the kind lost in transactions.
It's not my right to know,
But when you're gone
To where I want to know.
It's not my right.
It's my jealousy,
My feelings of ownership.
I have no right to know.
I haven't felt the blow
Of the velvet hammer,
But still I need to know.
Tonight I feel ownership
To what is not mine by right.
I'm temperamental, eliminating
One face while replacing it
With another. No wins!
Accountability lacks here,
Prevents coordinating times.
Some things don't change.

Divisions

Your conditions for love
Leave me reeling.
Were your position more puissant
My pen would lay down.
Home's center needs strong
Stances posed.
Oh, mirror, one day my
Reflections will revert rearward.
Your hard words rive deep,
Slashing my hand leaning on the wall.

Sonny Gratzer

The Fire of Wine

You tinkle when happy,
Your laugh good and natural.
It is a brilliant lilting sound.
It fills my ear, my heart.
My longing extends.
Your bonfire burns
My crisp leaves
As if I am nothing.
You don't know to deceive me.
You could but you merely evade.
Your grace and agility
Contrast with the wary fool I am.
Tiny chains hold weathered ovals.
They would bar your wine
Thirst from my room.
We will drink long entwined.

Questions

I don't want to be a grown man crying.
Who is my halo of emerald light,
My ray of shadowed gloom?
Who comes draping the lilacs?
Answer these things.
Who sets my heart in bubbled doom?
Who will act as the blue
In my month's double-moon?
What is this tempestuous
Side of your tender heart?
I glean bit by haunted bit.
My tags prescribe the pursuit
Of what will come to an awful end.
Successful hunts do.
Don't let me find you.
Stop me at the gates.
Gutting and skinning are indelicate
Methods of ending the deal.
Hide yourself in the thickets.
Let the season pass.
The dawn of first day
Glows hunter's orange.
A black purple haze lifts the sun
The way your brilliant black eyes
Lift my spirits.
Don't get caught.

Sonny Gratzer

Mars Dreams With Venus Aloft

Spangled nights when Venus
Sits atop the moon
Around the world in Petra Valley
Sun smoothes heaven's opposite.
The turning globe means my inertia
Will spin you to my blue moon nights.
Were I of good sense my fantasies would end.
Were I of like mind with you
Still our paths would not wholly merge.
Yet our disparate lives could brighten
With new lives learned in love.
Anon, precious, anon. The urge is great
But reality chains my legs,
Stakes me to life without you.
That I may have bits of you calms my soul,
Enhances infrequent encounters
And leavens my spirits.
I'm in the mood—recall the days
When I could not hurt—
I was invulnerable.
My growth rate was slow.
I know now what I missed.

My Guitar Lies

Cracks of lies split my ears
When you cry with my guitar.
Strings plucked agonize in destiny's screams.
Our journey strains in mountain meadows high,
Snow trekking suits tuned to Alpine winds.
Where are you going?
You don't know
Yet you rush to get there.
Slow before you can't be caught.
You slow the growth of time yet fail
To hear the potency of bandit's howling
Laugh above the high notes.
Listen.
They can be heard even with tiny ears.
You modulate and speak lowly, softly,
As if to calm contumacious children
When you speak to the masses.
I will be recalcitrant if only to have you
Speak to me with such passion.
Strum me, pluck my strings gently.
Create chords with your bitty fingers.
Hold my neck and play.
Sing your song
Of love to me
Today.

Sonny Gratzer

My Prayers.

I am raw to your well-baked breasts, kneeling in supplication
While red and blue women line my walls, begging for mercy.
My prayers need not be answered while the fig of life
Adorns my headspace, bewilders my nuance, disturbs my knowing.
I am breathing the life of the wicked because I am wicked in you.
I yearn for our togetherness while we have no chance at it.
While we pretend great things await. While mercy begs
Muscled haunches prove your mental worth
As no one makes gym time so valuable as you do.
You work out. You dictate to me how to work out.
You sacrifice. You bend the rules. You get me on my knees.
I pray for you. I beg for you. I pass your baskets of coin.
You answer me in the night when we pass our whispers
Through the thin night air, rasping for breath as we climb.
We are nearly there, dragging over the last riser together.
One last surge promises our effort's reward.

Leaning Lines

Simple gold jewelry hangs preciously
On your thin beautifully arched neck.
I ache to play it again, the music
Of your finger's sweet inverted melody.
Mountain's leaning lines bust into heaven
Seeing you as competition.
You are both magnificent
In profiled baths of mirrored sky.
Haunting hills owe me no passion.
My search ends with you sleeping
In comforting down.
Withered memories of youth
Pale fighting your elegant maturity.
Amber flakes touch your skin
Glowing in shimmering design.
Drips of hair falls soft on your smooth brow,
Minor obstacles to my eager lips.
My breath blows soft on your sweet skin—
Remembering.

Hunting in Starlight

Mia amica, you stride easily into my life
Like the day's soft entry over purple waves of mountain ranges.
Pure hearts are made during the magic of love
And the adrenaline of warmaking.
To feel the purity of each is to spend your life
Searching for them again.
With love, it is possible.
With war, it is impossible.
The rush of those loves is immutable.
The solemnity of those torrid acts purified in the deep,
Deep drops falling on tin-can roofs
Is as pleasant as sipping deck drinks in summer's
Flowering jingoism at Flathead Lake.
Pistils of wild roses bring the bee,
The nectar-hunting humming bird.
Tiny squirrels chatter loud at the soaring osprey
On my cliff of dreams.
Dimensions dim in the soft-coming night.
Generations hum in distant chords
Within night-running warning lights outboard—
Christmas-colored, leading the way.
Our trails are lighted by forming stars
Glowing in the heavens, western orange tints
Line the navy blue mountain ranges in its early dark.
Cougar screams break the forest's reverie.
Raindrops seek dust, creating puffs
In the unswept winding stairs of heaven's jewels.
Being below the bursting dam I push the turbo's edge.
Elk will bugle for me this fall.

Mountain Meadow Amore

I follow you and fill my tags
Forcing lines greased by lilies in my warrior dreams.
Fill my coffin with bones not mine.
Fill it with empty dreams not mine.
Fill it with saffron robes to ease my head into the box.
Let the color of your hair blend me into eternity.

Sweet Melon Carrier

Open your arms to azure skies.
Rub your crimson globes deep in pale green waters.
I am a cynic viewing my life as stale coffee.
Lift your toes through sage's green.
Aim for the heart.
Make your case in this life
Before time drains the essence
Of your womanhood, before my
Devouring crocodile jaws close
Shut, missing your breast
And nest of robin eggs.
Sweet Princess, release me from this entrapping tree.
I'm the gnome to your faerie.
Hear my coin of life jingle in the pocket's bottom.
Rub the bottle and dance in faerie rings.
Release us to the delight of magic memories.

String

Sentimentalists cover the backdoor
Refusing to get caught being open.
Objects elude my grasp when I reach
For the end of the hobbling string.
You don't assent, your snaffle too loose
To train you in my mendacious habits.
You see the traps I set,
Wily little creature that you are.
I want you set in your baffling ways as I found you,
Yet I try to entrap you, to hold you on my string.
You are not to be changed, trained to my reins.
Your free spirit needs its own track.
I ponder your freedom
And realize my own is chained
To an identity of you.
You are destined to remain untrained,
Free in your own ways,
Lover on your own time,
A spirit at the end of the string
Untouched.

Spring Step

Blended dreams elude shades
Ranging over plums of smoky mountain valleys.
Stacked mounds guarding high country plains
Reveal inlets through which tiny feet may tip.
Come here in your gliding machine.
Take chances for short-time gain.
You can't permanently sever grants
Though you sense the good,
The smells, the tastes of life
Awaiting you in the Five Valleys.
Sweet spring winds blow when you submit,
When you step giant strides in life,
When you fear not your future.
Let cool shade soothe our heated hearts.
Bring the mellow peach of your face to me.
Kiss the place you want your mouth.
Move with the strong ballet grace of tiny women.
Sail with billowed dreams to this shore,
This safe haven, a place you know to trust.
Hurry, bring peace to these valleys. Hurry.

Our Hearts Beat

My warming place is quiet, more than usual.
It is comforting to hear only my breath.
Were you here I would stop breathing
To listen to your young rhythmic heart beat
In tune with my own.
We would blush, your wide loving smile
Disarming me in a candle's soft glow.
I would blend my counts with your splash.
We would swim in the blood of our youth.
We would look forward to see the back side.

Your Weekends

Randomly I seek solace in tricky words you fail to answer
When I wonder how you fill your nights in my absence.
Noncommittal retorts with mischievous chuckles
Betray your nonchalance, your dagger in my side
Digging and twisting incisively, deeper with each laugh.
Sometimes you say nothing to thread the needle.
You need not say anything; we know the meaning.
My pains are secret even though the world knows them.
They are universal but I hide them nonetheless.
My schemes are neon bright in a gray world,
Personas revealed in such flashing light.
I am a lightening bug, a firefly, a bat with glowing eyes.
I am easy to see.
Nothing to hide.

Where Are You?

Black windows hide my soul.
Solid bricks consume mustard tints
When you give me sweet love.
Virgins are anathema in your fertile presence
When your Niagara flows.
Southern belles are old maids in your wake.
Symphonies are toneless in your string section.
Battles cease with wafts of your patrol.
Horse snakes crawl when you paint
Shadows in their stalls. You don't control
These episodes. They happen as you ski their slopes.
You arch like France when Huns invade.
You allow no discourse when I empty my ashcan.
You are alone when I light your path
With fireflies in my hand.
I lead you to fidelity's door
And want hands to knock.
I will answer.

Personal Angles

Dancing yellow waves turn
Blue in the orange evening night.
A large fish jumped there, or I wanted it to,
So it did, after the beasts hummed by, tippets trailing.
Colors mixed in the droplet of your changing eyes
Give fire's mix a bad name.
Vibrant reds crash in smoky hues
Spreading into clouds hung high.
Seasons tie together less than your whims
Spreading creamy as favorite tasty soup.
Waving holiday flags commemorate less
When you swing by, your sassy brassy prance
Dueling purple clad marching lassies.
Certain views are only seen from places
Others cannot go.
It's you I see through rising steam.
The face and place of Venus aglow.
Higher duties proscribe my offering
Details of sensuous sights,
But sometimes glistening lights
Sparkle off the sunlighted water
Reminding of magic evening delights.

When We Sleep

Where do you go when you are tired,
When your eyes flutter asleep?
Do you enter my world, read my books,
Paint my colors, salute my flags?
Where do you go?
Do you visit my ebony neck,
My mahogany back,
Do you pluck my flat-wrapped strings?
Do you sing the meadowlark's song in your sleep,
The sweetest bird song of all?
Does my brilliant peacock tail
Attract you when you sleep?
When I drag my tired feet
Do you let me lean on you?
If my lips moisten in the night
Do you kiss them?
If I meander in my dreams
Do you follow on tiptoe?
When I look back for you
Are you there when we sleep?

Responses

You rippled my thoughts,
Massaged me in eucalyptic splendor
While angels whispered our names.
Myrtle merged our sweat
And sweeter juices.
Where is there a kinder touch?
Your soft fingers were gentle,
Soft on my aching self.
Reach the limits when you want.
Fear nothing in response.
Release totally,
Abandon your self-imposed subtlety.

Rainbow

Morning's burgundy clouds portend
Chain breaks for the goddess's slaves.
Cottonwoods spin webs in my heart
During afternoon winds,
Claiming lost wages if I play the game.
Great thunderclaps acknowledge my aim
Of stripping you from life's wastes.
We shine together in every hour,
Mine the dark of storms,
Yours the sunlifting shine of day's open doors.
You exude soothing balm.
Stones turn to dust under your weightlessness.
Your touch smoothes my wrinkles.
Wild stallions submit to your offered hand.
Your grace is sumptuous in its altruistic mantle.
I see mine shafts gold-filled sifting
Through your painted fingertips.
Surging streams still when you wade,
Your skirt high to your hips,
A voluptuous net cast for my eyes.
I am caught.
You catch and release,
A new age of tempered dawn.
Colors in your eyes change
When you look at me in twilight's dimming.
Your name sings in the wind, blown
Through the leaves of my heart
When I connect with you.

Sing My Dreams

The last dream of sweet
Mounds grown on you
Complete a picture from early life.
You light my dark hallways.
You sweep my graveled mind.
You unlock my stifling cuffs.
Paint an impression.
Scrape my barrel's bottom.
Float my boat in tossing seas.
Mellifluous notes bend your strings
In harmony sweetly sung.
You paint and strum me,
An easy chord to make,
A canvas eager for oil.
Staffs lined hold notes sung by
Meadowlarks in my large pocket.

Bellicose Bread Crumbs

Who has built my flights of fancy
Into this, absorbing my faults?
The gray dawns of yesterday
Will be my life's work.
Something must remain.
Would the slip of silk on your waist
Hold me back from wanting you?
The grasper recognizes such flimsy trifles
As mere cinnamon covered crusts
Of thumb-thick wheat bread.
It lacks your sweet full taste.
Your defiant flag waves patriotically
In my attacking war winds,
Sifting through struggling starts.

Sonny Gratzer

Calefactions

My bows are bent, warped,
My arrows are soft spaghetti in flight.

What have we wrought? Do we get what we sought?
Were we better off with things forgot? Sing, my love, free and loose.

Angle kisses in our arbor put me in a libidinous state
Warmed by our calefactions.

Bowers filled with the likes of me
Though you've already formed your legacy.

Sooner than later we'll level the field
For all season's greetings.

Dreams

Why do my arms ache to hold you?
What gains made echo your call?
Earnest lives march lock step to nowhere.
Vacillating intensifies the worries in mind's eyes.
Sleep away your dreams, said the lady.
Sleep away your dreams.
The bugle's call to arms sent me away from you.
You turned to a foreign grasp of life.
Throwing swords at my shoeless feet broke
My will and caved me with bloodless hacks
Into unspoken mental tricks.
I bow to your goodness, your luscious taste,
The drips of our tears washing through time's
         beaten tracks.
When is the mountain too high?
Should I attempt to surmount your twin candy peaks?
Ice crystals grow in your eyes
If I don't warm your tender heart.
I will be your warming fire.
My torch will make your frozen water run.
I will mop your puddle of dreams.
I will swim in your dreams.
I will be your dream.
I see your face in objects below the pass
Where caravans of benign humped animals
Carry my message of hope.
Your valley of sleepless nights mesmerizes me.
I shade my skin from your exotic beam.
I am steeped by the wonder of you.

Suffering

Times past we loved greatly, not deeply,
Warmly, not richly, yet fervently, not impassively.
We melded into better beings, fill
The breech with empty smiles batted across fields of dreams.
Stifled lives regret spring's leafs plucked too soon.
The bloom of youth's countenance sways us not late in life
With tragic ends too clear.
I have seen ends before I should.
You, too, but your pain has not been deep.
You bleed not.
Your tears are painted
With the tips of humming bird wings fresh flown over honeysuckle.
Truth is deeper than the rouge of falsehood.
Tea leaves spell edges of boxed beliefs leaving hope failing fast,
Finding new loves in old places.
Giving rewound feelings lift makes small gods smile,
Tweak of fortunes found.
Bent stems bleed too, uncut but changed forever.
Where are the lost souls?
Hover near; help, my angels, my faeries, my batted dreams.
Deepest pain kills spirits as slivers of regret solve nothing.
Be strong, lovers. Be strong!
Suffering will, cried truly, make rigid your bones,
Strengthen and bolster resolve, broaden your smile.
The small gods and angels will smile.

Some Tales Are Different

You beat me with waves of your Oscar smell.
I know: I bought it for you.
Its pungency is more you.
We lip out wrongly putted through dripping bat shit
Fertilizing in white/black clumps.
Similar to your vision of our future—
More black than white.
What bridge do we take across the shimmering
Red stream of blood left from our wars
With each other? Do we wear our shields proudly?
Did we shunt the thrust?
Sweet cola brands the USA as overbearing, ugly even,
As capitalists sell our unique and fruitful style.
Your sardonic eyes scream at me
When I devour you, when I search
The depths of your family place.

There is no replacement for you in my affections.
You can't be replaced. You are and have been
In my head and heart too long.
A wisp of love living in hell
In this ragged, beat up heart,
Always and still, you were too good for me,
A class above.
Miner's sons feel the difference.
We knew our place,
We know our place.
Your food chain placement was assured,
An accident of birth—your own birth.

I know but I feel it myself. My God,
I am ready to pluck your handspun glows.
Vinegar eats my soul.
So go to hell, shame the honey tree
Defending daisies in foreign streets
Spread with orchid butter and chirruping sounds.
I long for you intermittently. I would
Have merely used you once.
Now I idolize you having learned my lessons
Watching young lives pass quickly into void zones.
This is essential, of the essence, land agents like to say,
A bargaining chip—a legal intimidation.
I want to intimidate you.
You spread yourself so thick.

Impressionism

Impressions left by you
Show my indentations
In your soft muscular self.
I am in shock.
You are so wrong for me,
Light-headed in a black world.
All around me it is dark
Yet your radiance leaves
Its impression.
You are silk to my sackcloth.
A bagpipe to my comb harp.
Plaid to my bland brown.
I am stamped forever,
Forged by your imprint.

Roundup

My foot is stuck in a cattle guard while riffs
And country songs are played to me.
Previews of future smells in wretched colors
Doom my olfactory sense when loping ponies surround me.
Barren stages sit ghostly, great thick black curtains
Subtly move blown by apparition's breath.
Fougasse attracts men wanting to be boiled
In their skin if barbs fail to deter.
Serpents wind my legs.
I can't move my frozen
Eyes in nature's beauty.
Your hair holds me down, staked by little men
In my dreams, your dreams.
My despicable self cuffs me to the cave's mouth—
Liberating me in deep waves of tears.
I'm reluctant to stretch, afraid my back will break.

Your Misty Eyes Touch Me

You desire me, you said, don't you?
I do, I said, always.
What good does it do?
You are there, I am here,
And there is no fix to our distance.
It is lost time.
It matters not.
I can be foolish forever
Because I know you care.
That's good enough.
I remain enamored.
My cells reek of submissive love
When death would do,
But I am saved from a maggoty end
By your pure bright beauty.
Your misty eyes feed me,
Nourish me, and enliven me.
I can't die until I have owned you
For a while. At least for a while.
You can leave me to a rotten end
But I must own you.
I have reached pinnacles
But yours is the highest.
I soared over mountains, medals fell to me like snowflakes,
I defeated warriors on their turf,
Yet you are my last campaign, my last conquest.
You should not let it be.
I would die then, to own you once

For all to see and know on my terms,
Not yours.
My feet touch the stars and I look down
At your sunny crest.
I uplift a spirit in you that
Needs the rougher me.
My skin needs to touch yours,
My heart to touch your heart,
My hair to tangle in yours.
Brushed wind would not be as gentle
As I would be to you.
Your misty eyes would twinkle like the heavens.
Your radiance would dim the sun
If you were with me.
My touch would blend with yours
Forever if you reach to touch me.

You Are Good

What flower
From my bunch
Lives beneath peach petals?

Suborned, wave-like
Through demigod's screen.
Graceful pollen pods burst
Blown, lifted beyond our grasp.

The moment flitted for us,
Wanting to be held, lifted,
Adorned as a brow wreath worn by angels.

What leaves are these,
What grasp is left, ethereal—unembraceable—
A wisp of love, and life?

You, frail wonder, are steel strong,
Are the firm hold on me,
On my arrow of love
Aimed for your petaled nest.

You smell
    So good.

You taste
    So good.

You touch

So good.

You move
        So good.

You are
        So good.

And I am lost without you.
You are my sequel and my end,
My continuance in things good.

        You are good.

Classified Secret

Golden black flecks of feeling
Leap from your beautiful eyes
When you don't want them seen.
I see them anyway,
Feeling their gentle, stinging
Rays pierce my core.
Soft seams of your skin
Meld with mine,
High hopes conceived.
Loving you is lasting love,
The kind that simply comes
without design or scheme.
I could not plan this
Comforting joy with you
Laying by my side.
Impossible to explain, different as we are,
Certain truths emerge.
Love is ours alone to keep,
Our secret, seeing deep
Inside each other.

Sonny Gratzer

Sleeping Bears in Flower Gardens

Petaled softness holds me tight in the dark
Of my mind's eye. Somewhere you lay thinking too
About the things we're determined to do.

Peach corolla garlands smell of you
When my sleeping mind gears that way,
Anticipating sweet new games to play.

Sensuous times await you here each day.
Times I believe will suit you well
While I wait to sleep in hoops of your spell.

Time is of the essence we know well,
And bright minds will ken
Waiting to come to an end well spent.

We'll see each other soon, no worries of our bent.
Hasten, faerie princess, with great expectations,
To the Land of Faerie because the bear awakens.

Wounded Souls

Bitter men hide hurt innards,
Slighted lives cope with antagonistic greats,
Self-thought high-stepping winners
Who should humble themselves soon.

Humans need expressions of emotion.
Arms waving, body moving, feeling,
Like a great conductor with orchestral explosions.
If you don't sense it, you're diminishing.

Harvested memories provide memorable bonfires
During Winter Solstice.
Warm thoughts decrease the ire
Once felt at relinquishing your kiss.

Happy times sweep the board
Clean and snow white,
Banishing ill thought toward
Those who think in terms of spite.

Sonny Gratzer

La Mia Amante

Short summer nights lengthen when you're not here with me.
Long winter nights shorten with you by my side, *la mia Amante.*
Paint me warm times tempered by a cool sable brush.
Let me see more of you, make your cheeks blush.
Time is important, we have little of it to share.
I must see you any time of night, or day, I don't care.
Not just in my silent loving dreams,
Give me time to revisit the shadow of our loving theme.
We'll never be through.
Why do I sense a measure of melancholy in you?
I need to know a time is coming
When I can blend with you in ways so loving.
If you won't let me be with you until Judgment Day,
Let me see you day by day.

Angels Decide

The end of lives hurt the solitary peace of never-ending bliss
While life and gaiety can't withhold harsh breath.
You breathe in my mouth, my ears, my neck,
An angel looking at me, grinning, holding back what I expect,
Unwilling to help, not unable, but sold on another's happiness.
Angels see so why can't we?
Do they know better than we do what is good for us or not?
An angel's daughter's breath is fresh in my face from years ago
While my own stale being the wind blew away.
The fit is not forthcoming, nor will it ever be,
This angel said to me.
I wish she wouldn't grin so,
It makes it hard to believe.
Aren't angels here to help, not grin you down to naught?
Why is my karmic pain so lasting?
Why do I pay so many prices?
Are my decisions so faulty?
Why incessantly repeat?
Give me some grace, some freedom, some time.
My pathetic dreamings can't make you mine
But your angel can.

Our Dance

Lonesome nights I dream of our dance,
The way we used the floor,
Or dream of times long before
We took a chance and I courted you.

We loved unforgettably, and we danced.
We used the whole floor.
Now I dream of times
Long before we took a chance and I courted you.

Our lives have changed, but we still dance.
We're older now, and wiser too.
But I still dream of what we used to do
Long before we took youth's chance, and I courted you.

Our hair is gray, but we still dance.
It won't be long before we part
But it will be just a start of our new dance
In a new place, a new chance, and I'll still court you.

Now you're gone, but we still dance
In my lonesome dreams we use the floor.
There are times I laugh aloud
At how we wowed them long before
We took the chance and I courted you.

Accented Rain

I kept your scent on me today,
Unwilling to wash it away.
I still feel your beautiful long hair
Brushing me so soft and fair.

The tender look in your eyes lingers still.
And if I can find a way I will,
To spend more solitary days
Quietly hold your hand in mine as it lays.

You chuckled in delight, teasing on hands and knees,
For you to feel fulfilled with me,
Flipping bands at me as I quietly laughed
Giving yourself so generously, a loving graph.

I can't see where my fervor for you will lead.
I crave to be with you as often as you will cede.
You foreordain more than I,
Come closer to me and we'll alibi.

I want to be your loving man,
To spend time with you as I can.
With you being bound to someone else,
Discretion is my promise.

Why am I tongue-tied with you now?
It's new to me I will now avow.
I honor everything about you.
Your spirit is in my mind, fighting the reality of what I can do.

Keep me in mind,
Know that my feelings run deep.
And know, too, solid secrets I'll keep.
After last night, tonight deeply I'll sleep.

My time with you sweet as your sugary lips.
I'll forget forever my former life's blips.
Your kisses more luscious than ever tasted.
Not knowing your lip's succulence, my life was wasted.

Opiate

My little anodyne princess, we'll struggle together
Reading, weeping, drinking, sleeping.
Loving each other and the good life.
Ends don't matter as much as going there
To live and learn and join ourselves
In empathic reverie, to hold true to what
Could have been; we now have the right
To close doors on age old desires.
Mistakes we'll make, surely,
But wining, dining in silk sheet's lining
Will help catch us when we fall.
Doing is better than trying—let's take our opiate now.

Breasts

I glean drops from the sweet
Icicles of your breasts.
I salute those soft mounds,
Those tipped spears
Swept away in smooth sliding grace.
Always changing, you direct salutes
To your harmonic twin globes.
I crawl to them,
To lick and taste them.
You turn, laughing
In deep-throated joy.
We are like that together,
Mirth one of our faiths.

Without You

Seasons lost, names dimmed,
When you died, I died within.
Sun shines still, the globe stays bright,
Where I live, all day it's night.
No home without love.
No home without love.
Candles glow, lamplights too,
Must I go on without you?
Rust leaves crackle, as does ice,
Your profile glows passed in rites.
Try again, oil rebates given,
Kisses sweet, home, home again.
Bent legs, mellow lights and tilted ghosts
Glow green on old fence posts.
Split sheets in tawny red,
My run is sweet and I feel dread.
No home without love.
No home without love.
Golden tones cover your body.
Stripped of soft blouses
Silk lacks your softness.
Your feet of oil were
Plumbed from untold depths.
When elk bugle autumn
You'll hear my approach.
The downside of summer
Brings you here—not at my bed—
But to me you will come.
Games we play once or twice post annum

Sonny Gratzer

At great cost delivering encomium.
No home without love.
No home without love.
Ice breaking into the sea
Leaves my heart pounding
To the bottom leaving space for me.

Resting Place

Your whispered silences bring
Howitzer sounds to my resting place.
My keen sense of serenity is cleansed,
Freed, stolen from me when you enter my place.
Lines of doubt cross the Missions,
Their highest peak as low
As I'm willing to go laid on my tarmac
Skim my waves.
Ride the crest we create.
You keep me there struggling for air.
My sun will set in the middle of the night,
My own age recorded.
Your mysteries are blue with heat.
Your firm gentle touch brands me.
I find no solitude in being alone,
Only despair in the Diaspora of my demons.

My Stove

Nothing emerges from this union.
Nothing is provided. You turn off the stove.
My cooking turns into garbage dumps.
I fail in my misery. I leave you
And nothing to change. I make large beliefs
Substitute for prayer.
I am alone.

I win alone. Who else can win for you?
It's our job to be alone, our fate.
We come in and go out that way—
Naked—jaybirds going back through hell.

What is the heat to me? Why do sunburns
Feel so good to my brown skin and hurt you?
When pilots fly do they see deeper into souls?
When divers submerge is their sea boiling?
You turn off the stove before my cooking is done.

When will a meal be filling, will it be on our next picnic?
Somnambulists grope toward the edge,
Searching for their night vision,
On a quest, like Indians on a cliff searching for names.
Why do you ask? What's in a name?
You turn off my stove.
I finish cooking.

Spare Me

Your calls demanding my sleep
Come in wee hours asking
For the guts of life
I'm not willing to give.
I know how it hurts.
I've hurt.
Now you hurt.
I don't feel good about it.
It's not fair.
You don't deserve this.
I didn't deserve it on my turn.
I admit I like you taking me
Away from my worlds.
You honor me and I deny you.
Your words are loving and harsh,
And you call me names.
I laugh. You are funny. You hurt.
I am the names you call me.
Renegade. Selfish. Hurt soul.
No truth to me, only flying versions
Of your hurt rainbow eyes
When you cry diamond tears from pressed coal
Of my mind. Only you know the joke.
I hurt you and I am sorry.
I am glad you know the rules.

Found Again

Sensuous tips
    Gliding through red strands,
Sliding to your lips, your hips,
    Your smooth cheeks brush my hand.
Silky soft is your skin,
    Glistening, eager to let me in.
Ardent intentions
    Have my attention
From the night
    I first saw you again.
No forgetting now,
    Losing our touch,
Time, too much of it lost,
    Found again, and I care so much.

But a Little

Wildlife's nocturnal cacophony blends strangely
With our sensual touch of cool skin.
My night eyes disguise my wicked grin,
As I know you see in the dark.
You see everything in the dark, or light, day or night.
Because I hide little.
Some.
But little.

We need no mask. We're not prone to sabotage.
No hooks or fades, only long straight drives.
We're weed free, from rich topsoil turning clods into
Towering pines where small creatures climb.
Hide the nuts, furry tail, hide the nuts.
Scurry and scrounge. We can't send motives into the wind
When garbled echoes cry our names.
Tomorrow sunstrokes kindle blood rhythms in real time.
My cliff is ready to climb. I have no barometer.
I have no need knowing my humidity is high.
My sweat filled the cold flowing creek
Where I laid myself for you to step
Does it matter I have no reach? Can I wail in panic?
Just a little? Let me hide a little.
Some.
Not much.
But a little.

Songs you sing torture me with their validity.
I fail you in so many ways.
You can depend on that, on my failure.

Sonny Gratzer

Throw your lifeline if it helps.
Perhaps I could reach it.
I would try.
Not much.
But a little.

Scare Me Away

I saw you peering from beneath the covers
When I left in the night; you pretended peaceful sleep.
Soul searching reminded us of promises made, of songs sung.
Deep inside—an internal close-up—we found the lies.
Scenes of things said and done wrong.
Innocence dispirited us, scooted the known away.
Limed veins spread curious spurts through leafy hearts,
My way of growing toward you, perhaps away as well.
A mere sprout of love, a seed waiting for water,
Buried in the internal close-up.
Smell me, Sweet One, feel the throb of blood flow.
Let me stink in your nose, let me fall after you cut me.
Tarnish your scissors with smeared life from my self.
Believe in our probable expansion, and live in me.
Stay the course—or run, but do it quickly.
Your watering thins my patience, but I grow either way.

Creeping Home

Sin-Sin on your breath and quiet with your feet
Tells me I shouldn't ask where you've been
So let me sleep while the midnight keeps.
Don't talk now, let my puzzling steep.
Tip your toes quiet in the night,
Quell your urge to hit the light,
Slip low beneath the covers
Before you wake your soon-to-be other.
Trees locked into Zen, even seeds
Growing on picnic tabletops have their needs.
Chirp high, chirp low, sing in pre-dark notes
Of mindless birds, sing your baffling responsive tones.
Leftist lights a 4th of July ago
Bend the sights as floating boaters go
Circling by—light ahoy—against the marbling sky.
Heading where? Speeding home?
Hurry, hurry before you're left alone.

Cleansing Sun

Dripping golf love scams in wrinkles
No one should have at this age.
You're true when it suits,
When your trust is pure,
When you lack anger,
When envy is not putrid green.
Soft sheen of ether skims off greens
When September sun strains my eyes
Low and eyebrow hard.
I can see into the sun.
Not many can.
I am not blinded to truth.
Squash my old rawhide body.
Tell it whole!
Edge me out of the dark corner of lies.
Brighten my day with honesty.

About the Author

A life-long Montanan, Sonny Gratzer grew up in Butte, Montana. He is a University of Montana graduate (1963—BA History and 1976—MFA Creative Writing). Following military duty in Viet Nam and various adventures, Sonny published *General Issue Blues, Viet Nam to Here: A Warrrior's Tour*, a book of poetry pertaining for the most part to Viet Nam and it's affect. He enjoys life, liberty and the pursuit of happiness, especially on the shore of Flathead Lake or on any golf course.